Report From X-Star 10

Laurence Overmire

Indelible Mark Publishing

Indelible Mark Publishing 2009

All illustrations and front cover photo by Laurence Overmire

Back cover photo by Nancy McDonald

Library of Congress Control Number: 2009926927

ISBN 978-0-9795398-1-7

6498 Lowry Drive, # 4
West Linn, OR 97068
www.indeliblemarkpublishing.com

For Nancy

whose love and support made this collection possible.

Also by Laurence Overmire

Honor & Remembrance
A Poetic Journey through American History

One Immigrant's Legacy
The Overmyer Family in America, 1751-2009

Captain's Log

Message in a Bottle

The television creeped in through the back door when we were on vacation. It stole into the living room disguised as a necessary component of a modern-day lifestyle. So we didn't notice it for quite a long time.

It seemed harmless enough. Kind of cute actually. But it began to grow. We fed it little bits of attention at first, but soon it wanted more. And more. And more.

We threw it scraps of idle moments and snippets of an hour, but still it grew and grew and grew — till huge chunks of an afternoon and evening, whole weekends and slices of terribly gloomy days were not enough to satisfy its need.

It spread its boxy fingers into every corner of the house. Up the stairs into the bathroom, down on the mantel in the den, then to the kitchen and the bedroom, even beside the baby's crib. And still it sucked away the hours, gobbling fortnights with a trowel.

We, desperate for some respite, gave it everything we had — our hearts, our minds and even more. And now this huge invasive caterwauling psychoblob of perfidious bizznobabble is holding an advertisement to our heads and threatening to take over the world!

It's too late for us, but if you get this message, please, whatever you do — run, hide, anything, but — Save yourself!

Before it's too late.

Nuclear Age

The child came into the world with a nuclear bomb
Hanging like a mobile over his head.

At any second

Every thing
Every place
Every body

Could be vaporized into nothing-ness.

What innocence is lost
When the mad grown-up world
Intrudes
Like a rapist in the night
And shoves a cold cocked revolver
'Neath the covers
In the crib.

Einstein Whispered

Einstein whispered
In a half-deaf ear
Secrets untenable to a cauterized world
What foul equations
Linger in dust
Light years hence on a black-holed road
Uncovered iniquities
Wrack the brain
Blood to wine and flesh to bread
We stumble on the square root of Truth
Divided by the remainders of
Sums uncalculated
Enchanted logarithms
'Neath a geometric moon
While smiling serpents
Bid us eat
Forbidden fruit.

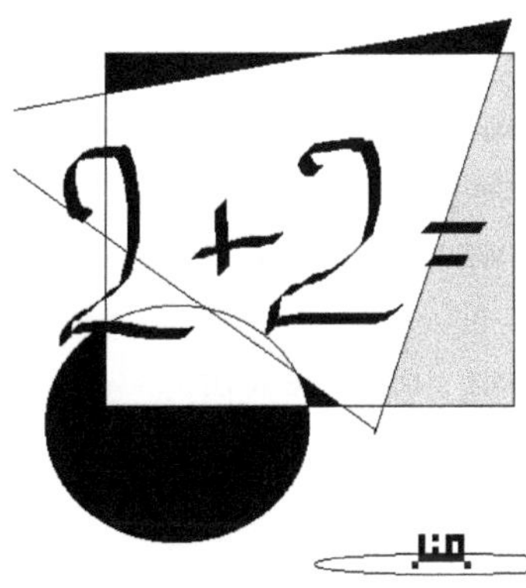

Report from X-Star 10

It was a strange planet we landed on
A contradiction of nature
Serene and turbulent
Profane, yet divine.

Beings of all size and form
Inhabited magical terrain:
Open sky and waterfall
Deep jungle and arid plain.

But even though their eyes
Deep-set in rather large heads
Appeared to be open
In sad, unfortunate fact, none could see.

In blind trance, they set about
Destroying, using, manipulating
Until what had been beautiful once became
Irrevocably ugly.

Even so, incredible as it may seem
They could not see the ugliness either
Instead building great monuments
In praise of, what they deemed

An extraordinary conquest of
Dirt and stone.

A TZ 4U

What is the value of a human life?
In the doing or the being?
In both? or in neither?

What is the value of your human life?
Something to consider
From the Twilight Zone.

Family Night

Atom and Eve

We are the holograms of our
Spiritual selves

Matter but a figment of a
Greater imagination

What is real seeming
Improbable

The substance of who we are
Impossible to hold.

THE EXPULSION

Great conquerors with a taste for blood
We tamed the land
On a mandate from an Almighty God we made
In the image of ourselves
Not caring to embrace the divinity of our own
Creation.

Like a beast that had to be subdued
Struck with saw and chisel
We killed the fighting spirit of the rivers and the trees
Blasting through mountains, pummeling the
Centuries-old layers of volcanic ash.

Drilled bars of iron in block cement
Plants and animals imprisoned within and without
Hope of ever being free again
Innocent, pure in the Garden of Eden
Crushed serpents

Under the foot of Man and Woman
So ashamed of hiding our nakedness
Our cained heads abled
For utter destruction, seeds buried in
Depths of soul soiled in the center of
Heart-beating Earth.

The Helix

We are programmed
With genetic code

Predestined to live and experience
Suffer, the world

Not freely willed
Our paths most certainly

Hacked
Out of stone and marrow of

Uncountable stars.

Lightning from the Genome

99.9% of our genes are identical
One human to another
What difference, then is
One-tenth of a percent?
Enough to justify
Hatred, jealousy, contempt
War?
In one-tenth of one percent
We lodge the miseries of the
Human race
Proclaim ourselves better and
Best
Conquer and divide
According to divine rights of
A primitive mind
Unable to distinguish
Reason from insanity.

Beastly Ideas

We humans like to think of ourselves
As being
Better than the animals
Smarter, and undoubtedly closer
To God.

Yet animals are forever true
To their God-given natures
Communicating well enough
With canny precision
In languages we are perhaps

Too arrogant
To understand.

Scientific Observation

Whenever you speak the truth
Someone will be offended.

Truths are not mentioned
In the casual conversation
Of everyday living.

They are purposely tucked inside
Little lies
That allow us to feel good
About ourselves.

Anyone who dares disturb
The social order
No matter how well-intentioned
Can expect swift retribution
The severity of which
Is in correlation to the degree of
Illness in the individuals

In question.

The Politics of Trees

I much prefer the politics of trees
They haven't got any, you see
They just grow
Minding their own business
Taking in the sun
Giving breath to all life
At home, their sturdy place in the world
Content

Until some fool human
Chops them down for
Kindling.

Gyroscope

To get to the truth
You must transcend words

You must transcend
Consciousness itself

Allow what is underneath
That great unknowable Hidden

To take what voice it will
And make the world

Spin on the fulcrum of its axis
The riddle burning in the center of

Its hot, molten
Core.

Beach Walk at Sunset

In the combing of the
Shore's sandy locks
The sun's slow plunge into the
Darkening sea
Amidst the natural breakage
Of stone and shell
Lies the tangled, twisted refuse of
Mass human consumption:

Beer bottle broken
Cigarette butt with a lipstick smear
Hairbrush caught in a spiraled fishing line
Dented soda can — where's your happy-go-smiling
Commercial now?

Rope without a purpose, untied
Loose end disappearing 'neath a two by four
For what? Or whom?
Q-tip, toothbrush, army man toy
An automobile's forlorn tire sloshing in
The surf, its balding tread tells no
Tales
Even an old, rusty air conditioner
Dumped unceremoniously here

On the strand where lovers walk

Odd, how the driftwood seems out of place

A child with his canvas bag
Takes up these things, unwanted stuff
His father watches well
They do their part, together
What look like shells in strange colors –
Red, green, bright orange, blue –
The young boy finds are plastic shards of this and that
Molded into some new marine-like form
Verging on the miraculous
Even the white bits of Styrofoam are almost
Unrecognizable, nestling comfortably with the
Pebbles and the rocks
The Earth somehow reclaiming these unnatural
Elements into the very body of her
Being.

No doubt one day
When mankind has long disappeared
The garbage of the past will have been
Re-made into something compatible and
Perfectly normal.

That time will come
The Earth will be cleansed
A comforting thought
For a father and his son
A mother and daughter awaiting their return
Despite what we humans may or may not do
The Earth will endure, going on as it always has
Forever at home with the revolution of sun and moon
And wayward, inconstant star.

Ode to an Endangered Species

Will you not leave us here too long
We have not paid attention
To squander the best of the world
A pity we do not understand
Ourselves
No more you fly in the wind
No more the buoyant ripples on a pristine pool
The splash of color in a worn-tore land
No more
The survivor's sad lament
But no weeping will there be when
Your perfect, singular form
Vanishes
The muted salting of a wounded Earth
And all that is and all that ever was will
In some way be
Diminished
For the loss, though unnoticed
Will be recognized
In the stillness of eternal night.

Less Than Infinity: October 12, 1999

Six billion.
Doubled in less than forty years.
Can you count a billion?
Nine zeros times 6
Means what?
Hands, fingers, stomachs, mouths
Six (6,000,000,000) billion
Elbows
Bracing one against the other
For whatever reasons
The Earth becomes cement
The sky ripped apart
The tiger, the hawk, the elephant
Die
Bones in a graveyard
Overgrown with weeds
Distended open-mouthed babies cry
Needlessly
Choking on air
Too thick to breathe.

Invasion of the Mouth People

The Mouth People
Talk, talk, talk, talk, talk
You see them everywhere
On the TV
In the supermarket
At the office
Everywhere the Mouth People
Are spewing toxic waste
Upon the minds of the unsuspecting.
Unfounded, silly ruminations and disingenuous
Cerebral bile are
Infecting the infrastructure of cultural sanity
Threatening to destroy the very foundations
Of civilized society.
Be ware.
You must sharpen the dagger of your wit
Defend yourself against the onslaught of these
Obnoxious
Orally-bloated creatures.
Should you, even for a moment
Let down your guard
Your reason may be blind-sided by insipid propaganda
And before you know it
Slowly
Imperceptibly
The Mouth takes over from the brain and
You become yet another of their minions
A babbling ideologue
Set upon the destruction of common sense and
The unholy imposition of
Absolute bull— derdash.

The Dawn of a New Religion

Greetings and good morning, my brothers and sisters. I am the Reverend Mr. Jesus Mohammed Elron Schwartz. Welcome to our Church, The Church of the Bald Procrastinator. Because we are a tax-exempt

organization, we make lots and lots of money without giving back a penny to the IRS. Sometimes government regulations can be a wonderful thing. Now some of you may be asking yourselves what it is we believe. Quite

simply, we believe in love – as it has been proclaimed in our holy gospels which were handed down to us by aliens from the planet Zorkon while they were being transported to a level just above human. Yea verily, we are

commanded to love one another. And we do. However, there are some people who are not like us. These people we can't stand. But we do love them. We just don't love them very much. It is our duty, the good books tell us,

to try to change them, and if we don't succeed, to be rid of them in one way or another. In fact, we envision a time when all people are the same, when, no matter where you go, you may take comfort in the same shopping malls,

parking lots, and fast food eateries, when life is so simple, people won't even have to think. For as it is written in Deuterlobotomy Chapter 5 verse 22: "Ignorance, is indeed, truly, bliss." And now, we would like to extend

the hand of friendship to you. We invite you to be among the chosen people, to be saved from eternal damnation, and to praise God with your generous offering. And please remember, all contributions are tax-deductible.

Baltdorf's Ray Gun

Took many, many decades
To build and perfect
The ability to annihilate
So necessary to protect
The safety of one's own
Civilization and people.

The enemy, of course, was
Constructing a death ray of its
Own
And the question was always
Who would finish first?

Who would gain the right
Through force of power
To dictate the way the planet
Should be?

And neither we, nor they
Could believe it when the Ray Gun
Was stolen by
A third inconsequential party
For whom anger was the only God
Worth worshipping.

The first ray destroyed a city
The second, a country
And the third, well...

This is what is left.
Could anyone have imagined?

I suppose not
Or we would never have built the damn gun
In the first place.

Mind Set on Stun, Captain

Look at life from a different angle, Captain
And you will find that the world
Is far more complex
And infinitely more subtle
Than the cross-eyed delusions of black-and-white detractors
Whose ill-conceived boxes of limited imagination
Condemn with ritual precision
Any notion outside the realm of their white-picket-fenced-in
Morality.

Say what, Spock?

"All right, Jim, so I am a Bricklayer."

Standing on my soapbox, offering books of
Socially relevant reform, I loudly proclaimed

"The pen is mightier than the sword!"
Whereupon the throngs, gathered around their

Video games, soundly ignored me
Slashing, thrashing and blowing up

Virtual enemies with the flick of a
Button.

Ed Would

The Past is wrapped around my neck
Like a sci-fi gob of alien

Goo

Sucking the life out of me
Present and Future
Seeping through holes in my skin

I need

Some laser of spirit
To shoot through my ego

Sever the hold of this
Scum-breeding figment of
My much too active

Imagination.

Plastic Bubbles

Chemicals are wonderful things
They make life so much easier
Do chemicals
Why, I love chemicals so much
I would want my son to grow up to be
A chemical and marry a nice chemical girl
From a good chemical family
And if you've got something against
Chemicals
Thinking chemicals somehow
Cause cancer why
Let me be the first to stand up and say
Our studies clearly show
Chemicals don't cause cancer
People do.

Big Fish, Small Pond

The corporation got so big
Swallowing little corporation
After little corporation
It finally swallowed — Itself.

The destruction was so vast
So completely global
It was impossible to figure out
Who to blame.

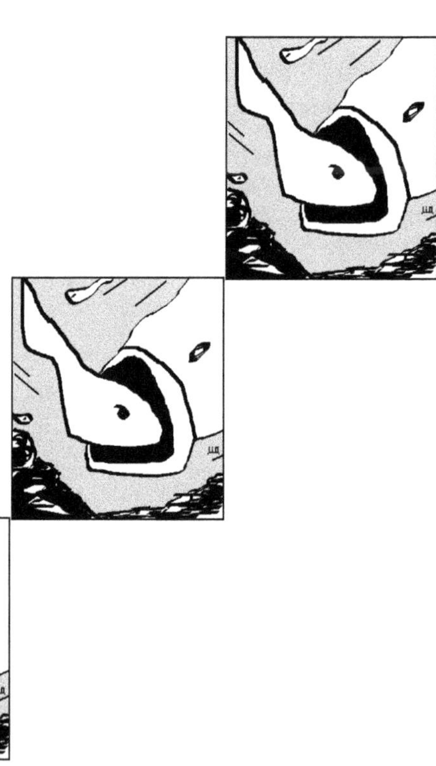

Alternate Universe

I am haunted by the man
I could have been

He follows me down every
Wrong turn

The blocked wall in a maze of illusion
His face indecipherable and yet

Necessarily contentious
The making of ourselves

Hanging in the balance
The choosing of each day

Critical
With time running out.

Hello, My Cyber-Spaced Friend

I'm never quite sure about
Cyberspace people

I mean, who are they, really?

You never meet them face-to-face
In the flesh
So they really don't exist, do they?

They're like characters out of an
Unknown author's script
And who knows who is holding the pen? Or why?

Cyberfriends? Are you kidding me?

How can you trust a fictional character?
When all they have to do is refuse to answer
Any entreaty, leave you waiting in cyber-limbo
The cold shoulder of neglect in the swift delete of an

E-mail.

What kind of friendship is that?

And most of these so-called people
Are usually as often nasty as nice.

I can't tell you how many unwanted barbs
I've taken to the heart
In an unwitting moment of
Clicking, without knowing, too soon.

Who are these strangers who feel they have the right
To wound for no apparent reason?

What's that all about anyway?

Does the impersonal nature of cyberspace
Allow us to be inordinately cruel?

No one to call us on our insensitivity
To our fellow human beings?

They're like hit-and-run phantoms
Who pass in the night

Leaving blood and bloodshed in their wake.

What's in a username, but a user?
A rose is a rose is a
catnapblue65? C'mon. Get real.
Just another Yahoo afraid to show his/her face
Dot com.

I'm not one to hide behind pretense.

So I have to tell you
If you want to be my cyber-spaced friend

I'm a little wary
A little suspicious
And more than a little on my guard.

Real friendship takes real relationship
The physical conjunction of mind and heart
Body and soul
Requiring depths of substance
That penetrate illusion

And make of the world
Its own solid foundation of a truth that
Really matters.

Techno-Man

I'm plugged in. wigged out. logged on.
To the wall.
Brain-wired
Through windows of intercyber space
Tele-marketed on airwaves of
High-tech no resolution
Toastered in a micro-waved oven
Ears popped corn-wise
My electric eyes spin in sockets
Juiced like a jingled julep
Sucked through the jargon
Of video laser loserlips
Played for a lackey
By big no-name hucksters who think
I have no will of my own.
But if I pull the plug
Now
Will self and soul re-boot
Or just be
(Deleted).

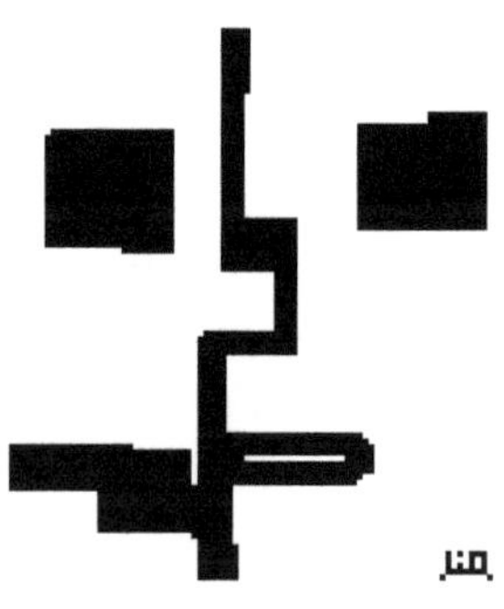

ORWELL'S WINDOW

From dysfunctional nuclear
Family, without relatives to

Balance, miles too distant
Contact rarely made, friends

In cyberspace, never met
Hardly known, dis-figured

People, like TV images
Not really real at all, so

Why not expose and exploit
Take without giving, use

Without caring, no sense in
Thinking we actually need

These fragments of our dim
Imaginations, instead to feed

Whenever and wherever
Desire compels.

Portent of Things to Come

In the Big Bang of her birth
Blood spattered across the walls
The doctor's violent hand lashed the tender behind
With a thunderous smack!
A scream erupted from the newborn throat
Gushing air
And spewing hot anger upon an insensitive world
That could so viciously
Rip life out of the guts of the void.
The scorching cries of pain burned through the corridors
Out into the night and
Deep into the darkest reaches of space
Proclaiming to the universe
"I am here!"

That's a Negative, Roger

No
The world is a No
No No
Don't No Why
No Can Don't
Double Negative No
No Yourself
No No No No No
Dodo do a No No
No be nothin
No be nix
No be wanka No be
No don't stop me now
Nada No no mo
No goes
No where
No why
No way
No how
Noooooooooooo dontellmeee No
No mo NO fo me
I don't No
No mo!

Picking Up Space-Age Chicks

I can feel the heat of your uranium eyes
Splitting my atoms into tiny particles
Of radioactive fire.

C'mon baby

Don't leave me hanging in suspended animation
Unloose your hot desire and
Nuke me with the power of your love.

Geeks in Love

FIBER

We forget that air
is a substance
we can't see it
but it's there
connecting everything

and everyone

With every breath
i take you in
give back myself
we are in touch
no matter how far

The distance an illusion
between that which is
not and can not be
separated.

ICE STAR

What tidings do you bring
Like Mercury from the gods
You fiery-footed herald of
The vast unknown?
How many civilizations did rise and fall
Since your last report?
How many seas have vanished
From the cosmic shores

Burned to vapor 'neath a million suns
And how many creatures spent their final breath
Separate and alone
On the brink of time?

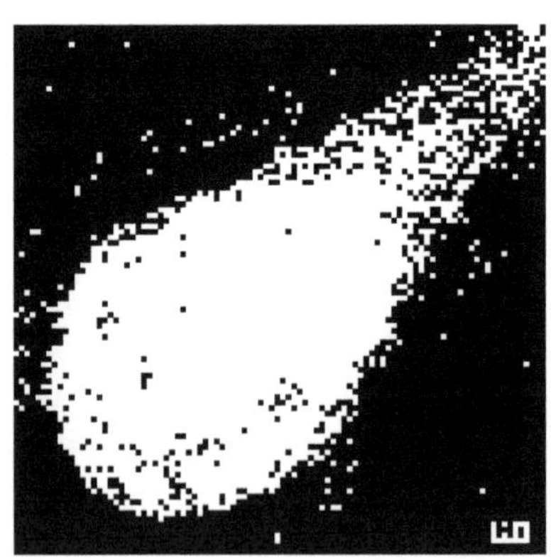

You have the answers.
You refuse to speak.
Or perhaps
We do not hear
Your foreign tongue.
Those flaming words enchant the eye
But miss the brain.

I cannot see you now.
You stray too far.
Afraid to touch this brittle Earth
Hurtling toward the gulf of black eclipse?

Send my regards
You vagabond prince
To those distant stars
Beyond the light
And whisper my story
To the sleeping moons
Nestled in their pillows
Of galactic dust.

And when next you return and
Find me gone
Listen for an echo and
Speak for me
To the wondering world
Below.

Anti-Gravity

Every day I need to spend
A little time with my soul
Connect with that inner space
When the world intrudes with
Scissors knifing through a Hitchcock curtain

The interior is forever
Impartial and wise
Knowing the secret of mountain and stream
The streak of a star across the sky

In the silence of still moment
Air in and out
The breath of life, immortal and sure
All that seems monumental
Becomes suddenly

Unreal.

The End of the Twentieth Century

Jesus walked into the Donut Shop
But of course no one recognized him
Why should they?
He hadn't been seen for quite awhile.
He sat down at the counter
Next to a couple of cops.
The waitress said, "You want a donut?"
Jesus answered, "Have you got mustard seed?"
"No. Poppy seed."
"It's not the same thing."
"A cup of coffee?"
"I don't have any money."
At this point, the cops were getting
Quite annoyed at this foul-smelling
Stranger with the matted hair.
"Hey you got no money, you can't
  come in here, okay, pal? Move it."
A businessman sneezed as Jesus
Walked past, out the door and
Into the street.
He disappeared of course.
And it will probably be at least
Another century or two before
Anyone ever sees him again.

Revelations 2000

Armageddon came and went
Did you miss it?
Right there as the clock struck twelve
Hideous demons with pointed heads
Bleary-eyed ghouls
Tongues rolling, curling, spewing
Hot bubbly gas
A thunderous whirl of sound and light
Ghosts flying through the atmosphere
Carrying the cobwebs of their dead careers
In hopes of resurrection.

O a piteous sight it was
The beasts lolling on the floor
Wasted in stupor
Waiting for some miracle
To change leaden living into gold
Fire from some angry god
To make sense of lost time
That cannot be redeemed.

There is only tomorrow
Hanging over our heads
Another sun, another moon
Another chance.

How about that?
Who knew?

Shooting Star

The soul connected
To the infinite
Carries the incalculable potential

To soar beyond
The confining limits
Of Earth's fatal gravity.

Expo 2020

Welcome to Biotech International Conglomerate Industries.
We breed and manufacture humans.
From testicle to test tube,
We are involved in every step of the process –
To ensure a high quality product, safe and long-lasting,
To meet the needs of today's demanding consumer
Society.

With Biotech, your satisfaction is guaranteed.
Our humans are genetically engineered
To punch time clocks without complaint,
To feel comfortable in suits and ties and other
Restrictive garments and
To perform duties with precision and efficiency,
With a strict adherence to the stern requirements of a
Healthy Bottom Line.

Here, for example, we have the Drone B-247EZ.
It comes in generic jean and work shirt, restaurant black
    and white
Or casual office ensemble for that friendly workplace feel.
With its creative tendencies effectively suppressed by
Tiny computer chips which stimulate pleasure centers
    in specific areas of the brain,
This model is most suitable for mundane tasks of limited
Skill, and perfectly willing to work long hours
For a minimum monetary allowance.
Raised on a continuous diet of insipid, voyeuristic
Television,
The Drone B, as we like to call it, is vapid and

Suggestible with
A dogged ability to follow instructions without thought
or question,
A perfect fit for the discerning employer who knows
How to increase profits and
Dramatically lower costs.

Now over here is our masterpiece of Biotech vision and Design:
The Corporate model A-642XE.
The X stands for X-pensive.
Just kidding.
Notice the commanding line of the backbone,
The strong arch of the forehead, and
The formidable protrusion of the jaw.
This is a human that won't take "no" for an answer.
Programmed with state-of-the-art negotiating skills and
The very finest in Machiavellian principles,
With the Corporate A-XE, you can rest assured your
Company will be in the forefront of successful
Takeovers and mergers for many years to come.

These, of course, are but two examples of the many
Fine products we offer at Biotech.
Whatever your needs, be they social, sexual or political,
We can create that very special human that you have in
Mind.
Please feel free to consult our sales representatives who
Remain at your service — on call — 24 hours a day.

Remember, at Biotech:
We believe in people, and people believe in us.
After all, we made them that way.

New Bottom Line

I'm not a communist. I'm not a socialist. I'm an
ethical capitalist.
Is that an oxymoron?
Is it possible to be a salesman or a businessman
with integrity?

Or, to put it more simply,
Would anyone buy a used car if you told them the truth?
These are difficult questions.
But shouldn't someone be asking them?
We've raised our children to compete.
The dollar is the prize.
All is fair in love and — just about everything else.
So is it any wonder the field is littered with losers?

Ethical capitalism.
The profit motive works. No question about that.
The problem is

Greed.

Greed is the knife that stabs deep in the backs of one's
fellows.
Self-interested profit for the few too often
Reaps untold suffering for the many.
The community of humankind is laid low in shame.
The harmonic balance of the Earth is

Disrupted.

Where are the visionaries to lead the world?
Powerful and influential men and women who see a
Future inclusive of all,
Those who understand
A dollar lost here and a dollar lost there
Is a victory not a defeat,

When brothers and sisters and children yet unborn
Remember with gratitude
The painful sacrifice
And honor the difficult

Choice.

Ethical capitalism?
Is it possible?
Of course it is.
Life is evolving.
New generations recognize
Money is just a plaything.
The new bottom line is

Humanity itself.

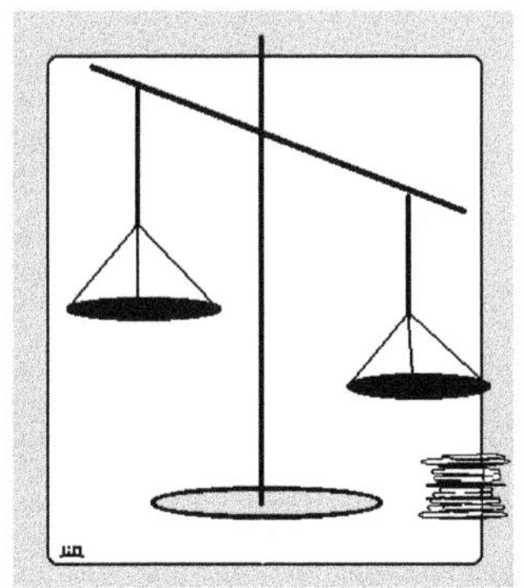

I KNOW A DOT

a speck in the universe
of what is and was and what will be
you know a dot
the President knows a dot
even Einstein only a dot
all of us know these little dots
all of which combined
can't come close to knowing
the totality of dots
that make up this exquisitely intricate
matrix we call

The Big Picture.

Optical Illusions

We wrap mythologies around our brains
Magicians' blindfolds
To trick our eyes into a certain way of seeing.

They shape and limit our trespass upon this Earth
Hurtling us into conflicts of our own magnificent
Ill design.

Our petty grievances languish in the bowels of
Succeeding generations
Laying waste to the promise of an innocent child.

Only the final blunt thrust of Death's indifferent sword
Cuts through the Gordian Knot of lies and
Stops our tinkering hearts from beating.

Questions

Without answer.   Dimensions.   Unfathomable.
Perceptions.   Inept.
Perplexing paradox.
Why
Why
Why
How to make sense of the bloody mess
We are
I am
You are
Out of whack
Find the center
The center
The center calls
For clarity.

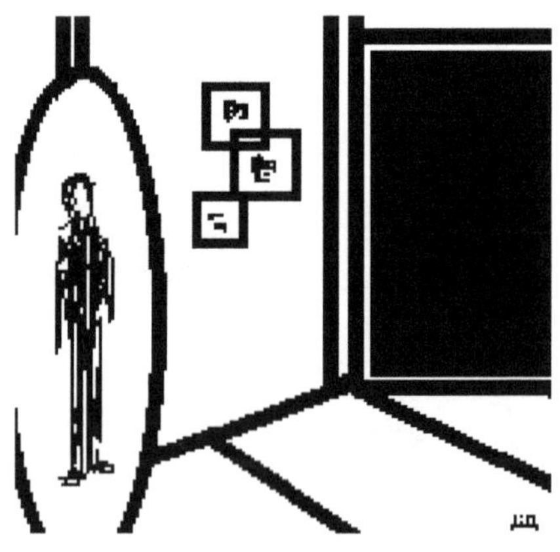

Is there
Somehow
Someway
Somewhere
God
Or are we
Just
Accidents
I haven't got a clue
And neither do you

Despite illusions and delusions to the contrary

In essence
We are all
Lost
A swirling enigma of elemental matter and matters not
We have but a fraction of a millisecond on the cosmic clock

This little life

Why
Why?
Why not
Embrace the mystery
Shatter the locks of heart and mind and sense
Open the door to the soul and

Dive
Into the black hole of the riddle
Awake and aware
In the beautiful darkness
The incomprehensible gravity
Of eternal
Wonder...

A Theory of Everything

If we could find it
The scientists say
Would make sense of
All That Is
Perhaps
To know the Mind of God

Imagine

Strings of consciousness permeating
This world, vibrating with symphonic precision
Eleven different dimensions leading to
Who knows where, from out the wormholes of our
Yesteryears
Our limited senses incapable of knowing

Those worlds we cannot touch or see

Yet, are we left alone on this desert island Earth
Theories to hold our illusions intact
Impossible to measure with scientific rigor
Willingly suspended in our own disbelief.

Maybe the Trees

Maybe the trees have lost their eyes
And the wind its wicked wisdom
The sand sifts through the glass
Unnoticed
The rivers cry in the dark phase
Of an old moon
Hear me, O Sun
Give life to the branch
Soil to the root
Fast water, graceful rain
A rising tide to wash away
Sorrow
We must emerge
Together
The upheaval of a great mountain
Through stratified rock
A peak of glistening snow
To claim the heavens as our
Own.

Real World

I seem to be slipping from the real world
the world of making money and paying bills

I've grown uncomfortable with the ritual
of going to and fro

unmindful of the journey
the play of grasses in the wind

I seem to want the solitude
the earth upon my hands

the stillness of the water
the quiet of the night

I seem to be maturing
a fruit ripening on the vine.

The Assurance of Children

I give you a promise

The promise of morning

No matter how dark the night

There will be day

The sun to dispel all fear

Fixed, at the center of the world.

Point B to Point A

The Big Bang was
Not the beginning but the
End of

What had been, and in the eons since
Fragment by atomic fragment
A new universe arises out of the dust
What was past is present once

Again
Relatively speaking
As of matter, of course.

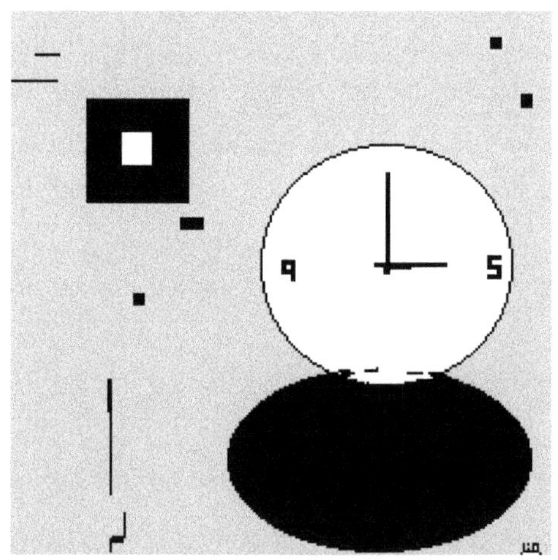

TOWARD

The mind of Man is evolving
In slow, deliberate process
Opening, not closing
Expanding, not retreating
More knowledge
Deeper understanding
Greater awareness

The old ideas that separate

One from another
Fall in the dust
The wind passing through the bones
No grief for the lost
A new grass rising
Roots embedded in fertile soil
To suckle in the splash of sky and rain.

Quantum

The physics of possibilities.
Sub-atomic world.

What's happening within us will
Create what's happening outside us.

The universe is mostly empty.
Atoms are not things, they are
Tendencies,
Matter completely insubstantial
Like a thought...

Think about it.
All things made up of thoughts.

The fundamental truth:
We are all literally one.

In quantum theory, you can go back in time.

The mystery unfolds in waves of consciousness,
The spirit, the observer, witnessing all.

Be in the mystery.

Reality is our possibility, day be beckoning day
Can we change it? Can we alter it with thought?

Think anew.
Make different choices.

The possibilities are endless.

The Rock

The rock was in my way
A huge immobile mass of gray
And I was determined to move it
One way or the other.

I shoved it and scraped my palms.
I kicked it and stubbed my toe.
I pushed it and strained my groin.

Finally, I went back to the house
Brought out my sledgehammer
And just as I was about to strike
The rock spoke, saying

"I am the Earth
and you — you are the root that grows
within me, drinking the rain of my
tears."

Don't ask me why, but I put down my weapon
And decided to go around the rock instead.

Viewpoint

The astronaut
tethered by a line outside his ship
circling the blue opal Earth
resplendent gem gleaming on the black cloak of space
turned his eyes
to the light-yeared depths
beyond the farthest stars
and said
"Forgive us
  for being such fools."

Climbing back into the O_2 chamber
he sucked his plastic straw.
Even the slimy green liquid
labeled "Peas"
splashed into his throat
like a symphony.

Clarion

The future is won or lost in the war of ideas
As we gather here today, our words flying into
The ether, they make war with loftier or
Meaner configurations of syntax and vocabulary

Out of this linguistic soup, making its way
Through a billion brains and
Five billion more
Half-starved stomachs

There are those few who take action
Those very few, for good — or for evil
Who dare to take a stand
To do something to

Change the world.

Where do you stand?
While the world passes you by and day becomes night
Twice as dark as before the last
Break of sleeping dawn

Before you've had time to
Set the alarm, pull the curtain, and rise up
Out of your much too comfortable
Skin.

Time Capsule

Will the ink
Pressed to the page
Remain
Indelible
Centuries hence when
No one understands
The meaning of blood words
On black paper

Who will know
What thought passed through
The fingers holding
A blunt instrument
To the crooked forehead
Of eternity

Who will ask why
Something wasn't done
And not done, lost
Never again to return
To the birthing place
Of origin
Where possibility became
Its own answer

Let the ink dry
And let its song
Sink
Slowly
Like the moon
Caught in the drift of
The mountain's long shadow
Deep in the crevice of
Darkening night.

ACKNOWLEDGEMENTS

Grateful acknowledgement is made to the editors and publishers of the following anthologies, periodicals and web journals in which poems in this collection first appeared, some in slightly different versions.

A Little Poetry, "Gyroscope"

Art Villa, "Optical Illusions"

Autumn Leaves, "Maybe the Trees"

Bellowing Ark, "Fiber"

CER*BER*US, "Big Fish, Small Pond"

dash 30 dash, "All right, Jim, so I *am* a Bricklayer"

Eclectica, "Nuclear Age"

The Hinterland, "Less Than Infinity"

Megaera, "A TZ 4U"

MiPo Magazine, "The End of the Twentieth Century"

no alibi press, "Expo 2020"

The Oracular Tree, "Ode to an Endangered Species"

Outsider Ink, "The Dawn of a New Religion"

Pink Cadillac, "Point B to Point A"

The Poet's Porch, "Revelations 2000"

Poetry DownUnder, "Ice Star"

Poetry Junction, "Report from X-Star 10"

Poetry Soul to Soul, "Lightning from the Genome," "Shooting Star"

Pulse, "Real World"

Seeker Magazine, "New Bottom Line"

ShallowEnd, "Mind Set on Stun, Captain"

Short North Gazette, "Ed Would," "Plastic Bubbles," "The Politics of Trees"

Wired Art from Wired Hearts, "Atom and Eve"

World's Strand Anthology, "Alternate Universe," "Beastly Ideas"

ZZZ Zyne, "Message in a Bottle" (1st Place Poetry Prize, 2004 Barnes & Noble *Fahrenheit 451* Contest)

About the Author

Laurence Overmire is a writer, educator, actor, director and genealogist whose award-winning poetry has been widely published in the U.S. and abroad in hundreds of journals, magazines and anthologies. He has performed on stage, film and television on both coasts and in between including the Broadway production of *Amadeus* and the network television soap operas *All My Children* and *Loving*. He also served as Executive Producer of *The Writer's Lab*, a non-profit organization in Hollywood to promote quality writing in the entertainment industry. Laurence received his MFA from the University of Minnesota and is a strong supporter of arts education, having taught and designed programs for *Lincoln Center Institute* and *Manhattan Theatre Club* in New York City among others.

Raised in the bleak expanses of suburban sameness, he regularly escaped into the otherworlds of Serling, Bradbury, Asimov, Wells and Roddenberry. Now more than a half-century old, he lives in Oregon, where he hugs the trees, talks to the ocean and laughs with the coyotes. His home is not far from where the famous Willamette Meteorite once plunged into the Known World and made us reconsider our place in the Universe.

www.ingramcontent.com/pod-product-compliance
Ingram Content Group UK Ltd.
Pitfield, Milton Keynes, MK11 3LW, UK
UKHW020136250726
13967UKWH00002B/687

9 780979 539817